Selected Poems

of

Kyriakos Charalambides

K. Χαραλαμπίδης

translated by

Greg Delanty

Greg Delanty

SOUTHWORDeditions

First published in 2005
by Southword Editions,
the Munster Literature Centre,
Frank O'Connor House, 84 Douglas Street,
Cork, Ireland.

Set in Garamond
Printed in Ireland by Colour Books, Dublin.

ISBN: 1-905002-09-2
www.munsterlit.ie

This book is the sixth in a series of thirteen published
as part of the official programme for Cork 2005:
European Capital of Culture

Cover Image: *City Interior* by Cormac O'Leary Acrylic
on paper, 23 x 16 inches

Cork 2005
European Capital of Culture

Grant Aided by
Cork City Council

Comhairle Cathrach Chorcaí

Acknowledgements

I wish to acknowledge that I couldn't have achieved these translations without the advice, expertise and patience of Gail Holst Warhaft.

Some of the translations were published in *Southword, The Stinging Fly,* and *PN Review.*

Contents

Turtle Hunt

You don't catch turtles with a fly rod.
They appear around 9 p.m. on the sand
dragging trawl nets, drawn by their own course.
Puffing, they slice the beach in two
and dig to a depth of about a foot;
they lay their eggs inside.

Quite a crowd turn each turtle shell
upside down with long sticks.
When they chop off a head, they're surprised
that the heart of the turtle throbs on
for such a long time.

The Dove After The Flood

The dove unfolded its wings, set off without shillyshally
to wherever the joyful sob
of its cooing led it.
Embarking, he saw the silent lake.
Nothing was familiar.
He traveled in the morning, wings spread
until he spotted masts; spars of wrecked trees.

In an age where there are fewer angels
than today angels flocked around
this messenger.
They were jealous that this dove
could manage the flight paths of the earth
with his little eyes and could dawdle
or return according to his mood.

But he
welcomed the wind since he couldn't see
the silver underside of the olive leaves
unless the wind blew. That was his job: ah
cut a twig and wing it home to that great
floating house of Noah.

Icarus

The sun
followed the contest of Icarus
high diving
into his grave,
losing the radiant glow.

The sun turned pale,
the sea made a pact with the sun
and she kept the pact,
neither of them in a panic.

The sun plunged beneath the sea
where Icarus fell, but couldn't come up with the lad.
The sun emerged again at dawn
hoping to retrieve him some day.

Each Time There's An Injustice on Earth

Each time there's an injustice on earth
the rumpus in heaven is something else.
The archangel asks, with a smile,
"What's all the hullabaloo about?" His battalions reply:
"Our eardrums are killing us, we can't take
that ruckus…."
"Oh fellas," the archangel replies,
"It would be wrong to bar the way
to what exists. That's how it is, God help us!"

The First Step

"Wounded Pride"
is usually your own ego
mixed with a smidgin of kindness to ourselves.
After all, what's more human than to make your bed,
sulking for some other reason.
Lose yourself in work, the brief

immortal zones within the kingdom of Mutability.

Cain

And the lord set a mark upon Cain,
Lest any finding him should kill him.
Genesis 4:15

1. He searched about. He found no one.
   They were off at work. He didn't know what to do.

2. He rambled into a garden,
   he hacked down trees,
   he raped a woman,
   he drowned three children.

   He cast an old man into the river. Defied his own
                                                 life.
   He became the Lord Corrupt, King Strife.

3. He announced war,
   defeated his enemy.
   In his fury he killed his friends.

4. One day he decided to rest.
   He pitched his tent on a mountain, began chanting.
   The wild beasts performed for him.

5. Grasshoppers came from far away. In the settlement
   there were rumors that he'd suffered greatly as he
   raped women, drowned children and threw the old
   man in the river. Finally, all the friends he murdered
   gave Cain their blessing.

6.The people came to see him.
   He hid in his hands
   as soon as he heard footsteps.
   The wild animals laid down at his feet.

   The settlement brought him clothes,
   offered him water to wash away his filth.

   They were all united.
   They beseeched him to love them.

7. But he recalled how much he's suffered on
   murdering his brother, on raping a woman,
   drowning three children, killing his friends, the trees,
   an old man.

          He went away to live
          on another mountain
          and hunch there.

8. And the wild animals came to him again and licked
   his wounds. He beseeched them to let him die faster.
   Doctors came from all over the world to study him,
   but he set the animals to guard him. Cerberus stood
   foremost among them.

9. So, Cain's life closed. He judged himself and died.

10. His mother, Eve,
    — six hundred years old at the time —
    wept ancient tears over him,
    just as she wept mournfully,
    six hundred years earlier, over her own ugly deed.

He Who Walked on the Waters

The message came at dawn
to some elderly fishermen in corrigals:
"Christ is coming over the waves.
He loves crayfish and sea urchin soup."

Crabs and turtles get together,
form themselves into steps to help him climb
down off the waves onto hard sand.
When everything is hunky-dory
the table is set for supper.

But he had to head north
to connect with his tired brethren,
those who weren't already petrified to death from cold,
thirst and hunger. He had to spread
his beloved word to all the children of the world,
taking care of them.

He'd even make a stop on the moon
to take samples of the new rocks
and ponder the fate of sweet folk.
He'd find, if he were lucky, Einstein,
Alexander the Great, Homer, Persephone,
and all the other good ones fortunate enough
to walk on the water of yore.

His eyes were fixed on their particular sign,
as Cain's was on his forehead, and he was not worried.
He'd take the mule from Cyprus.
The saddle was made in Damascus or in Epirus,
the bridle in Bratislava, the rest
in Copenhagen.

And so He said goodbye,
His wide sleeve waving to the little crowd.
He set out for His determined destination.

They brought him back in no time.
He stumbled, they said, in the river
wondering at a blue butterfly.

The Trunk Trembles

The trunk trembles in the heart of Regina,
the leaves tremble among the doves,
the hawk trembles on the leaf-lips.

Great Voice, Great One, hidden as you are
in the ox-skull of a snake scanning the horizon,

look at the clouds surrounding the dead
and the birds on the stave of electric wires.

Your car on the Green Line is torn between
that verdant line and the Venetian line
— brothers on opposite sides.

Facing you, Salamis,
searches for a new hideout. Engomi to the left
is trapped in heartless light.

Sea power braces the oars.
Gold coins plait the waves;
Poseidon fetches them out.

Achaios spotted Salamis, desired her,
a naked inhospitable woman,
her hair a flock of sheep.

With a leap he yoked her to his horse,
bent and kissed her, planting cities,
palaces, arenas, theaters, market squares.

This landscape is enchanted.
Time loses a tooth now and then,
the grinding wheel turns slowly and steadily.

With a rope you can lug
a town on your back. To rest,
hang it on the branch of a tree.

She can leave, if she wishes,
but she stays.
This naked woman who became the arch
of the aqueduct—the waters stir.

Bad news. They kidnapped her, the town.
They took the next town and the next.
The children slink up out of their hiding places.

Taking the City

Wanting to capture the cradle light of my city
I snag that difficult phrase of Dante *la materia e sorda.*
The mountain city, wrapped in a dusty cloak,
secretly spurs my childish cunning.
I'm not afraid that the world around me
is draped with an exquisite
old fashioned wrong.
I delight in its gasping breath, light
like life shines golden on my face.

The stone-throwing war of the stars
spits black blood, the chariot
of the sun's daughter is dragged by the hair.
I hold back the darkness of night.

The commentating days come and go.
The doves ignore the dividing line of Attila.

Confused matters fly to the place they're reborn.
Unadulterated time stoops towards them.
The town registered in the telephone directory
observes the sea and the cultivated trees.
Buses negotiate the line separating the town,
enslaved no-go routes and towns writ on their forehead.

Ochre tears flow down the forgotten mountain
beneath the stone.
The verdant, unconquered lawn of the sky
is in the song of two or three birds.

Ardhana

Half of the courtyard
— not a stone of any of it was visible
in the old days—
glared blankly.

That was just half the strangeness of the dream.
Our good neighbour's trellised grape vines
looked towards our house.
How could our neighbours go on with things
when some foreigners partied
in our yard?

The strangers looked at him, raising
their chins to the heavens,
signaling no.

He contrived on another occasion
to enter the courtyard through a rip in the dream.
He slipped in via the spare room.
A Turkish woman was drawing water from the well.

It didn't occur to him to ask why she was there.
He just took out his familiar handkerchief,
the sky-blue one, and wiped his brow.
She turned quietly and without a word
signaled with her hand
as if to say: "We're not to blame,
we have left everything the way it was.
What can I do for you? If you like, come in, have a
bite."

"This meant, Kyriakos," said the man, my friend,
who entered the courtyard,
"that we'll never go back to our village.
Yes, it's tragic, but we're better off facing it
rather than living in the darkness of hopeless hope.
In my dreams I approached our house more than once
and found a way
to cross the border, transported there,
ironically seeing the house
as I never saw it in measured, peaceful times.

I wanted to go in,
but the foreigners wouldn't let me.
I couldn't leave
the house in my dream.
There was nothing else to do, but wake up."

The poet listened carefully,
smiled and measured his words:
"If we let Ammohostos slip
from our grasp,
we'll also pay for it one day;
this is true.
Either we take it now,
or that's that.
We'll never get it back.
It'll be an illusion to think
that it will still be ours
just because it looks the same.
That'll be worse. It'll be as if there are
guards there
blocking off the routes of memory,
forbidding us to enter the gate
even in our mind.
Despite all this,

let's go on the town,
let's lift a dram, a toby jug,
to your poor village, Ardhana,
on the slopes of Mt. Pentadaktylos.
Let's drink, Sir Toby, to its health.
Atlas continues to carry the universe on his shoulders.
Time passes and everything disappears.
The sun will dissolve in a haze of silk.
Tomorrow will give birth to other monsters.
And, who knows, maybe I'm crazy,
but perhaps you'll enter your house some day."

Kore

In her mind she models the plasticine sun
that shrouds her betrothed.

Each morning she wakes,
his shirt hangs on the clothes peg, adorning the air.

She is dark, with curly hair,
plump hands and sad eyes.

Everyone knows in the village that she presses
his trousers with an iron, heavy as coal.

Child With Photograph

A child had a photograph in his hand
and a photograph reflecting in his eyes.
The photo peered upside down at me.

There was a crowd around him; the figure
in the little photo had large inverted shoulders—
and in the child's eyes smaller shoulders,
even smaller hands.

He was in a crowd of others with lists and photographs.
It got to me the way he held it upside down.

I went to him, passing posters and lists
of other peoples' loved ones, archways to voices
that were iced and silent.

The photo had to be of his father.
I inverted my head sideways to see the head
of the missing person. The boy's head was upside
                                                    down.
I was reminded how the jack, queen or king
are turned right side up on one end of the card
and reversed on the other end
as the boy stared up at me.

The Apple

Picking the apple from the basket
brought to mind the rosy apple
of her child's cheek. Even now
he might be rotting
in jail.
The poor lad wasn't more than seventeen.
He hadn't even finished school,
nor gone into the army. He wouldn't kill a fly:
he was so polite, timid and innocent.

She put the apple back in the basket
recalling (they seemed so vivid to her)
other mothers like herself under the Turkocracy.

No one really gives a damn about her child
except for her, and the thousand others like her.
God be praised, there's not a word
for all the petitions and official statements,
for all the committees and UN envoys,
for all the politicians and government officals,
observers and votes, obligations and engagements,
conferences, solidarity, exhibits and funds.

Everything is perfectly organized to a tee
with conviction, special auditoriums, records—
Yes, the motherly State takes care of all.

But the apple, the rosy apple in the basket.

Sparrow

Death snatches the leftover seedling
of beloved remains, here
and on the other side of the border.

But when, instead of leftovers, the sparrow
finds the mountainous corpse of a man in the frost
the bird wishes he was an eagle;
only such a powerful creature
could manage the heavy weight,
grasping the body with its talons.

The monstrous seed frightens
the lightweight sparrow.
He's not sure what he's going to do with it.
'Let tomorrow take care of itself,' he tells himself.

The sparrow clips the air,
arriving at the courtyard of a sheepish village house.
He counts the flock. One is missing.

It dawns on him,
patching things together,
that the body lying in the frost,
set out from here.
The parents say little,
the father chain smokes.
The sparrow wants to tell them not to wait,
that they should change their clothes and their hearts;
but that, again, would simply be concern
about tomorrow. The sparrow flies.

Of the People of Olympia

Day drowned in coolness. The mother from Olympia
goes to her daughter-in-law, Vassiliki, and says:
"Michalis, I'm sure, he won't come back;
marry, my girl, you're a flower at your age."
How do you know, mother, where did you learn this?"
"Premonition assures me, it's a year since he died."

The daughter sheds her black, gets into white,
walks to the church as if to a funeral.
She gives birth to child, names him after the dead.

The Tyranny of Words

To justify their actions they even changed the meaning of words.
                                        Thucydides

"I have already said that there is too much tyranny of words on this island. It depends, quite plainly, on the Turkish army's arrival in Cyprus. Invasion means different things to different people."

                                        Sir Ian Gilmour

His snow-white palm
darkly catches the stubborn rain.
A hare pops out of the bushes and lets on
its observing the lettuce.
Suddenly it steals our show and vanishes
into my heart clenched with tentacles of pain.
His breath reeks of tobacco.
This hare arrived in a helicopter.

At 1.15p.m. he landed in Larnaka.
"He came to observe", smiling all round
while behind his head
nestled his royal pimp.

He came to see. Carnations pop open
with the beat of the music. He strolls the foundry
of words with hammers and tongs, the devil himself.
Drinks are served before the meal's even finished.
They shake hands.
Ianus washed his hands.
What mother gave birth to him, what iron lady
patched him up into a prince? He handed us over,
our dirty linen, our so-called friend.

He forgot the callous on his foot
as he strutted around, smugly smiling.
Six years earlier, on the 14th of July,
I believed in that smile.
Another day made it to night.
It took five nights to enter the twentieth darkness.

Ships lowered their hold
and vomited.
Pirates who were about to turn gardeners
took Morfou, picked lemons from Lapithos.
Fruit sellers sell prickly foreign merchandise
on the terraces of Ammochostos.
Six thousand dead (unsung in our history)
nourishing our fields. They call insistently
for justice, if that's what its called, if it's something
that exists in the knot of innocent hope
and memory.

But Sir Ian doesn't fall for such things.
He's read Thucydides and Plataeans.
He's a fellow of the colleges.
He acknowledges the Greek world,
ancient Greek as the fulcrum of the West.

He bows before these things:
Kourion and Apollo
nicely set up in the Episcopos Base.
in the Dekeleias Base
the waves of history are chosen.

Without beating around the bush
he says "Oh Cypriots,
if you want to live in this situation
that you've landed in, you better think

about fitting into this box.
They have the key, we the bones.
They have the courage of heavy weapons,
helmets, chains,
the deafening racket of combustion,
and probably, if our sources are correct,
they chalk up a little collateral damage."

For our own good he said it clearly:
violence doesn't know how to give birth to the lie.
The lover of truth is born out of violence.
He was clear and brief as he became
the angel of death waving the symbols of victory.
You want food? First, sit down
and we'll discuss the terms of digestion.
Don't provoke your guardian angel; O
the Guarantor Power will get angry if you push her.

They tied your hands behind your back one morning
and gave the knife to someone
who'd teach you to bow to their orders.
You spout words, mouth about the invasion.
You've never been tortured, dragged by your lapel.
Your lips quiver uncontrollably, staccato words.
Thousands upon thousands
come to visit you and you simply scratch your behind.
Was that gratitude? Your words are ambivalent,
distorted and the like.
The not-so-bad and the bad rub up against each other.
Take a look at the Oxford and Cambridge dictionaries.

He says: "I'm off to work. I didn't come to interfere.
We'd place our good offices at your dispoal
if we were asked for them.
I fill my bag with evening fruit,

new wines, gold coins and terracottas."
He spoke, gave the head of state a push
and rose high —
deriving angel from anglo,
playing with derivation.

In the game of words, politics,
one crowd pulls on the oars and the other
steers the boat and waves.
This spleen-seller from Britannica
shrouds even Pleiades' brightness.
He was born in a thatched house. He remains poor.
It's not really his fault. Others made him like this.
God, perhaps the Creator will take care of him;
the economy of the world, Sacred Justice.

Ardhana II

I didn't know how to speak Turkish to her.

"Do you speak English?"

"I understand."

"Is this my house?"

"This is your house."

I began to weep in my sleep. The tears of farewell. My wailing woke me in a nutshell, Pylades. My bed was soaked in sweat; the dream dripped from the ceiling? Both of us see it, we know it, in fact we live it: "Our army is lost!" Nothing more, no boat in sight, no shore, no house, my comrade.

And yet the gate was the same, the bodreen the same, the pothole the same , the terrace, the oven, the tractor, the sheep pen. Yet I couldn't relate to the house. I didn't recognize it. I stood awkwardly in my own yard. If you'd seen me I bet you'd have broke down in tears.

I wasn't at home anymore in my own courtyard, in my own village—a stranger without any peace in my soul.

"What sayest thou? You were outside your own house and you didn't know it? Really?"

"It wasn't mine anymore, no. The house I was born in, Pylades!"

And indeed I asked her: "Is this the house my mother gave birth to me in?" And the Turkish woman answered me: "Yes, this is it."

How strange. How could she know this was the house where I first saw the light of day? How could she have been so certain?

Dying in Alexandria

A month after his death
speeches were given in order:
Greek, French and English
then Italian and Arabic. Of the lot
the dead poet favoured Arabic.
He already reckoned
that the characters of all the other
nations would fade,
— the cities would disappear,
the palaces and emperors,
all that his poetry survived on —
and that the Arab copper would hold out.

Arabic would remain.
It would be something like Greek in the age
of its expansion through the Egyptian desert
(the sound of copper is worth a bomb).

Before he kicked the bucket he realized
copper would also be melted down in buckets,

                         dispersed

in a thousand different ways. He said: "We only saw
her gown's silver coastline;
the swell of her chest rising eastward,
drowning us."

Now it's late, even for our death.

Story With Horse

Sometimes they spot me galloping on my horse
above the sky of Lefkosia.
Run and see, they tell me. I don't see.

But one day, strangely, I saw
what they were on about. Don't imagine
I'm talking to you about the likes of Pegasus.
It was a strong, chubby, wingless horse
with a bridle
as heavy as hail — Heavens, I who never rode a horse,
was off to the races.

From earth
I hailed my heaven-sent self.
Such an ass never paced the universe
since this rider
gave me a wild
fierce look. We were thrown together.

However much I try to lift
my appearance and my spirit
this rider circled me, put the fear of god in me.
He threatens me with his spiky knout
that had a moon in it, or swollen sun.
But I — seeing the others
cheer him on with handkerchiefs,
fattened lambs and a lot of jingles —
plucked a reed from the marsh,
somehow made it into a lance, a terrific spear,
and pierced the horse as he came alongside,
toppling the horse.

If you were a mother you'd wail
for the fallen son,
for your thrown brave bucko
who had to stand on his own two feet.

But I approached him in front of the king
and swiftly finished him off, so they wouldn't say
they saw me galloping on my horse
above the sky of Lefkosia.

Heading Eastward

Waters of Cyprus, Syria and Egypt, beloved waters of the homeland.

C.P. Cavafy "Return from Greece"

Alexander, these things are so obvious
they're invisible. Listen to me,
it wouldn't hurt you once in a while
to listen to me. In the old days you were king
before you fell from your high horse, before the river,
even before your coffin was filled
with honey. I think I can remember it, but you act
as if you've forgotten, as if it's not in your interest.

Really, where were you when we sunk your body
in the mouth of the Nile, and later concealed you
in the most secret treasury of the desert?
You know better than we do what
the meaning of homeland is, and what the meaning
of the mountains' language and
the sea's hidden beauty are. Nature helps you
each morning to measure the disputed skies
over you, while Northern Epirus, Ionia, Pontus,
the conspicuous distant island of Cyprus
reap endless love.

There are two ways of looking at it,
one is to see,
the other is to visualize with the eyes of the blind.
When you wake at midnight to the long-suffering
search for home

the latter would be better. Perhaps it's that world
people find themselves in Homer-ing
further south and further east
towards Egypt, and Syria.

Greco-Roman Civilization

On a verdant plot by the river
stood the hippodrome of Corinth.
There, Nero of Nemea, Captain Tamer himself,
deigned to test his strength,
or rather, rack up another victory.

So he mounts his chariot,
impetuous as ever, the unbeatable
Roman emperor charges off.

Bad luck; one of his steeds
suffers a sprain, but immediately the Greeks
replace it with another stalwart stallion.

Bad luck; his wheel buckles
and the hotshot Greeks intervene
and fit another wheel to his chariot.

Bad luck; the harness comes undone
and the horses shake free and stampede.
But the good Greeks, especially
all those competing with him,
immediately pull the reins of their chariots
and their horses brake.

Then the mighty emperor
descends to earth and crosses
the line on his own divine legs.
Thus he finishes first, as always,
sans his chariot—and so what?
He was a born conquerer,
unflinching before all peril.

The Greeks who are wise to such things,
madly cheer such a mighty feat.

If he weren't Roman, he'd like
to be a Greek certainly—he wishes
it seems, to flourish
in their logic and sound judgement: their applause
deserves a decrease of taxes,
the laurels they crown him with are worthy recognition
of a Roman citizen, certainly.

But not, by Zeus, their prolonged
thunderous ovations—the way they're going on
they'll walk off with the kingdom.

Invitation to Supper

I

It was as if God were to invite you to His heavenly Supper and you say "Thanks, but I can't, I'm fasting" or "I've just eaten."
"Come, if only for a drink, a coffee, a little fruit."
"I can't unfortunately. I'm expected elsewhere."
He urges "Come, just keep us company. You don't have to eat. Your company will be enough."
You answer "Can we take a rain check?"
Weeping bitterly for you he cancels the heavenly Supper. Everyone, planning to attend, quietly gets into their cars and slip away. Night shrouds the world in snow. Not a virginal foot ruffles the outskirts of heaven. A cockerel crows.

II

Other souls burn to attend the Supper — they yearn for it with all their hearts. They hesitate out of fear. Their own awkwardness scares them. Perhaps they turn their faces away, not being much for hobnobbing.
God continually goes out of his way to politely invite each of them,
— no, no, no.
He tells them to come here, come near, come share my light and breath.
But it's His eagerness that unsettles them. Who told the Lord it was they who wished to be the first and best at His table? They're so hungry. It's been months, years since they tasted food; months since they kissed and embraced their own and others.
Never let it be said that God didn't try to sweep them

away to his Supper and honor them, tearing doors and veils down in order that they and their retinue could steal in.

He draws them into his house, as always, with philanthropic pushiness. He beckons his slave and instructs: "Take these invitations and compel any soul you meet on the road to enter in order that my house be full." If I take the wings of morning, I'll take you with me—that's what the psalm says.

The slave goes forth, but trips, falls in his haste and disappears.

The Lord of the Supper waits. And, the days, the months, the years zoom by. My god, says God, now what am I going to do?

He fishes out a rag doll, the oldest, the most faded one from his childhood. He places it on his right hand. In the name of the Absent, the Hungry, the Thirsty; in the name of the indivisible holy Trinity let us begin to do justice to the delicious victuals.

In Aramaic

I wrote for eighty years
in Aramaic; who'll do it justice?
Who'll recognize how I gave myself to it,
studious as a child? Eighty years!

I wrote my songs in stone
—writing on parchment
didn't exist then.

Eight thousand, five hundred
and three handmaidens sang the Aramaic songs
from memory. The songs were embroidered
with folk tales, rattling stars, hair that shed dawn
on bejeweled buckles of night.
The mountains were nursed
in the songs.

But now I've come to a cul-de-sac,
the cul-de-sac of Aramaic, the whirled nest
of the nightingale lies by the wayside. The myriad tears
of these depressed, severe songs are lost.

In a short while, in less than fifty years
they'll ask who I was, where I hailed from
and why I hung on to a dead language. What   incited
me to take up the wonderful path
of a lost lingo.
Whose dantá are they in your laimheen?
Why did I decorate my mouth with ribbons
and roses long gone?

And, since I won't be able to answer them
— the answer will be long lost by then anyway.
I'll remain with the nightingales flying
from carved borders of faces, from archaic things
found only in museums.

I'll follow my path like one
whose thirsty land and well were drained
in the name of some foolish stitchers
who hid their flock
under the great dome of a tolling lost tongue.

Spoon Sweet

I paid a trip to my own place
to see who I am. I went and stood
at the bitter house, near the ditch.
A woman in a headscarf brought me water.
She offered me a sweet desert. I thanked her.

She plucked fruits from the Garden
of the house of my desire, shining fruits
of all kinds bursting at the lip,
soaked in the sweet balm of grace,
in the communion of shared gifts.

I thanked her. I got up courage and requested
to see inside my house, if it was permitted.

"Certainly, it's permitted," she said;
"You can see the bedroom also."

I entered, seeing my framed mother look at me
from the wall. I abandoned
shame and begged to take
my mother, poor thing, from Troy.

"Hell, take her." she says, smiling nicely,
"What can I do now I know?
To be honest we thought she was an actress
with all those flowers surrounding her,
with the grace she holds that parasol,
and, oh, that braid."

Certainly, it was worth mentioning also
that dainty gloved hand
reclining on the sofa, but what can you expect?

How could she know how many centuries
flew past until we reached the syntax
of the spoon sweet? A big question.

That the woman permitted me to enter
my family home was good enough.
Let's not go further and get her narked.
The only thing I wish: to have permission
to see again from time to time
the sight of the house of my longing.

Death's Art

King Cambyses, that Persian hard as granite,
was mad to humble
the Pharaoh Psammetichus,
his prisoner from Egypt.

He ordered that his old enemy
be placed in a cage of burnished silver
and set high above the Avenue of Lions.

The Pharaoh's daughter was paraded before him
lugging a water pitcher and with her breasts exposed
to torture him even more.

But the Egyptian remained a silent monolith,
his eyes fixed to the ground.

Cambyses, obstinate as ever, ordered
that the son of the pharaoh be bound
and savagely dragged before his father's black eyes
on the way to being executed.

Still Psammetichus gazed stubbornly
at the ground, his silence imprinted
with an ant's humility, a snake's wisdom.

A long procession of shackled slaves
were filed before him.
A sole servant
was the only Egyptian martyr.

The pharaoh broke into tears seeing this man,
his daughter and son too much for grief, beyond tears.

See how the Pharaoh prisoner
was so schooled in the art of death.

The Gods Amuse Themselves

With a little sky and a little sea water
the utensils of the gods are washed.
The paper cups don't need washing.
On the day
speed and dexterity are preferred.
Besides, the gods of the Upper World,
green by definition,
know what's behind the whole show.
Only one god,
dressed in human clothes, visits
the Delphic oracle from time to time.
He's gets a kick out of playing
with the embroidered report of the Pythia.
He doles out ten mina, the head
of Zeus on the front side.

I'd also like to point out the backside
of the coin,
but don't want to commit blasphemy,
especially since I declare myself a poet
which I owe in part to him. When I was born
he gave me a hand. So, I'll say no more
of the general guff of the gods,
their wine goblets and their wonderous feats.

Candaules' Wife
To Stavros Petsopoulos

Poor Candaules wanted to teach his friend, Gyges,
a lesson in aesthetics.
He asked Gyges to behold his divine wife
naked as she got ready for bed.

You can say the like of this is foul.
How does this differ from offering your wife over
for money to the first person that happens by?

Still, I don't think that's quite right.
Firstly, Gyges was the most loyal
friend and brother of Candaules, secondly
Candaules had a high sense of virtue
and restraint, worshipping
his heavenly wife,
seeing her as a star.

Gyges was his best friend simply,
his trustworthy confidante, his bodyguard.
He wanted Gyges to realize
the measure of his love for his queen.

"When I tell you that she is the most beautiful
woman nature ever gave birth to, I'm not convinced
you get the extent of beauty
with mere words.
If you wish, my friend, and your heart can bear it,
come and see her with your own naked eye,
she being naked too. You'll know what I mean then."
Gyges acquiesced, seeing
nothing would satisfy Candaules
except to behold her unearthly beauty.

Everything was to be on the sly.
Gyges would hide at the door that led
to the bedroom. From there he could watch her
remove her garments one by one
and happily lay them on the chair
with a delicate frolic.
You'd swear the gods were peering at her. She'd pour
her fancy garments off as if they were oil, intoxicating
wine.

Candaules' nightwords were on the ball,
she lit up the whole place
with her marble body's grace—she dazzled
the surprised heavens.
Gyges closed his poor eyes.
His heart was shaken.

His mistake was that he didn't withdraw silently
just as he had entered, breaking the agreement.
She sensed he was there. She didn't turn away,
but lay down to sleep in the arms
of her husband Candaules. (She reckoned
she'd let on to be oblivious).

The next day she woke and summoned Gyges.
In front of the servants she addressed him
as if in some folk tale: "Make up your mind
to kill your superior and take me
as your wife along with all his riches,
or else be slain on the spot; choose.
I give you my body, my flesh. I give you
the kingdom of Candaules, or
I give you the choice to kill yourself. These
are your only options; you saw me naked
and there's nothing more obscene to me."

51

The unfortunate pair decided
on the execution of innocent Candaules.
Ever since Gyges first saw
the vision he was motivated.
He killed Candaules dreaming
of the perfumes of his wife,
the vials and sweet fragrance spilling
from the vial of his soul into the bedchamber
as Candaules beheld his wife naked
beside Gyges.

Nitocris, Queen of Babylon

She achieved much
for the good of the people.
After a great deal of ingenius consideration
she initiated bridges, fortifications, diversions
(we are speaking of river diversion).

Before she died she designed a clever place
for her tomb above
the central gate. Out of respect
nobody passed beneath her body.

She added one other safeguard
over her tomb.
It had the air of augery.
Over her grave was the engraving:
"When some king is short
of funding, let him open my tomb,
but only if necessary; otherwise
leave well enough alone."

For sure nobody raised a finger
to despoil the tomb.
Besides, doves nested there.
"Mylitta" was branded on their wings.
But the impetuous foreigner, Darius,
bade them open the tomb of Nitocris
(mostly, I figure, to gain access
to the forbidden gateway).

What did he see when the tomb was opened!
Not a penny—just bones
and a note that read:
"Money grubber, you wouldn't have opened this tomb
if you weren't such a character."
Being a cultured man
he shuddered,
interpreting it as a prophecy that read:
"You have opened your own tomb."
He ordered his guards to reseal it pronto
and to fetch back the birds.

The Second Voice

All his life he separated art from life
(he thought art was higher than life)

but now it's the reverse
(ah, the scent of flowers, sweet redolence of Easter)

he realized he made a mistake in thinking
(but to think is human)

that the present tense of art is superior
to life and its future
(difficult things keep you up late,
but the thorn remains and ceases to hurt)

and the crisis arrives
(or crisis or understanding?)

if life ain't life anymore
(now that art ain't art anymore)

what is he to do, how go on?
(he'll see with poetry for a companion).

Potiphar's Wife

And Joseph was a goodly person and well favored.
                                        Genesis

Petefri, the chief chef and eunuch,
wanted to prove to himself
that he too could have a wife.

He said to the Pharaoh " If I can cook up
erotic dishes, by Horus, I have a right
to partake of the dainty titbits of life."

He was rewarded with the most desirable slave
of the palace. Now he too had a lovely dish.

Petrifi dressed her up in gold,
set a scarab at her neck.
He fastened a downy chastity belt
over her exquisite diaphanous belly.

He was overwhelmed with joy and power.
He went on cooking his master's ducks.

She withered, faceless and inviolate,
envying the mummies,

until one day Joseph came along.
He was handsome, twenty years younger than her,
forty years younger than her hubby.

He stood like a frigid Hebrew rock,
knowing duck-all about Phaedra and Euripides.
All he was concerned with was
his honor, and the cook's Egpytian corn,

the cook knew more about that
than the misfortune of his own wife.

If God could have intervened
he could have told the cook what to be careful of,
but as per usual God remained neutral
even though he sympathized with the woman.

She weeps and entreats him to stay
with her. "Take my heart, give me
your clothes, make me feel human again, Joseph."

But nope, Joseph was virtous as ever,
bound to the strictures of his fathers
and to the key of trust.

The Horse of Artybius

"Onesilus, my amour-bearer,
What do you think?
Artybius, the Persian general
rides a highly trained horse;
it stands on its rear legs and expertly
strikes and bites
with its teeth.
Which of the two
would you tackle,
the horse or the rider?"

"My king, I'll do whatever
you bid, but
since the gods have set both
against the Greek race
I'll be open about my opinion—
the struggle concerning freedom."

"You, as befits a king,
should fight a glorious general,
go head to head.
God forbid, if you were killed,
defeated, at least you'd die
by a worthy hand and cut
your followers, your servants' grief in half.
It would be more correct for us to face our like,
slave versus slave, an underling with the horse."

These were the clever tactics
of the amour bearer from Caria in Salamis,
to dodge facing the Persian General.
In his enthusiasm
the king didn't notice his strategy,
the servant manipulating
his freedom with the ethics
of servant and horse.

The Death of Alexander the Great

Do myths poison
the truth of history or not?
There is no other way to learn.
Take Alexander, for example. That selfish chap
planned to conquer the whole kit and caboodle:
countries, people, gods and the underworld.

It's difficult to understand the chemistry
of the demons if you haven't drunk
from the Styx. And so,
maybe the servant
took the bitter cup of Alexander.

Iolas, the chosen, hid the frozen
poison in the cleft of the horse's hoof.
Aristotle ordered him
to be careful not to stumble
and spill the stuff.

The plan is worth mentioning: Iolas organized
the drinking session with one of Alexander's lovers
(he was the Persian, Medios of the downy hair).
Iolas and Medios slunk into history
mixed up with the poison.

When Alexander drank the mythical wine
to the bravery and health of the twenty
invited guests, he was well aware
— this is the important point — that fourteen of them
were involved in the conspiracy.

Honouring Hercules, he raised the cup
stoutly as Socrates, and drank.
The half dozen men outside the plot
separated to the left and right of him
Crying *Evoi evan* and other bacchanalian chants.

But is was writ that their leader
would die as soon as he raised his cup.

As to the cause of death —
the doctor's opinion: malaria.

Tears For Twenty-Five Years

*For twenty-five years they mourned for another person because of
a mistake of the authorities. The new tragedy came to the surface
after the disinterment of the remains of the second lieutenant.*
From a Cypriot newspaper, November 1999.

They wept for him for twenty-five years,
his pure innocent features. At least
that's what they thought, but then they learned
that the man they wept for was someone else--
he silently accepted their tears,
unable to tell them what he knew
(besides, their mourning suited him).

When the earth was dug up
and the broken note of the truth rose
to the surface, the people felt bitter;
for a quarter of a century
they lamented him, but
if they had only turned their heads a little to one side
they'd have seen him unshaven and unwept for
curled listening to them on his bed.

He walked alone for twenty-five years.
They didn't catch a whiff of him
(this accident of life suited him;
in heaven your external appearance doesn't matter
a great deal except
if you're a wizened crooked old person or deformed).

Now that his sweet face
emerges from the pallor of bone
they weep for their own all over again,
for the man who fell for the winged
birds and the heavenly garden.

Notes.

pg 18: "The Trunk Trembles." *Regina* is a female heroine who is symbolic of Cyprus. *The Green Line* is the line dividing Greek Cyprus from Turkish Cyprus. A large part of Salamis is under the sea, another part is covered by forest.

pg 20: "Taking the City." *La materia e sorda* translates to 'matter is deaf.' The Green Line, the line dividing Greek Cyprus and Turkish Cyprus, is also known as 'the line of Attila.' The telephone directories produced by the Telecommunications Authority of Cyprus include telephone numbers that 'are not in service temporarily because of the occupation of the area by Turkish forces.' Buses, that managed to drive out of the occupied areas kept the names of the villages they came from, the villages of their former routes.

pg 21: "Ardhana.". The poem arises out of a dream related to the poet by his friend Andreas Marangos, the director and actor, who is from the village Ardhana now in Turkish Cyprus.

pg 24: "Kore." This is a type of traditional sculpture representing a female.

pg 28: "Of the People of Olympia." According to the unwritten code of Cyprus, a person who loses their partner is expected to marry again within a year.

pg 29: "The Tyranny of Words." This poem was written after a statement made by the British Deputy Minister of the British Foreign Office, Lord of the Privy Seal, Sir Ian Gilmour who arrived in Cyprus on April 19th, 1980.

pg 33: "Ardhana II" Based on a second dream of Marangos. See note on 'Ardhana' above.

pg 50: "Candaules' Wife" See Herodutus, *Histories,* 1, 8-12.

pg 53: "Nitocris, Queen of Babylon." See Herodotus, *Histories,* 1, 185-187.
pg 64: "The Horse of Artybius." See Herodotus, *Histories*, 5, 110-112.